LABYRINTHS

Walk and Color a Finger Labyrinth©

By *Marcia Raff*

Why Walk a Labyrinth?

Labyrinth walking is an ancient practice used by many different faiths for spiritual centering, contemplation, and prayer. Labyrinths are also used in a non-spiritual way and are walked just for fun and exercise. It is a walking meditation when you enter the unicursal (one way in, one way out) path of a labyrinth, taking slow deliberate steps while quieting your mind and focusing on a spiritual question or prayer. Walking a labyrinth creates many benefits such as reducing anxiety, lowering blood pressure, reducing insomnia and enhancing fertility. Regular meditative practice leads to greater powers of concentration and a sense of control and efficiency in one's life. Dr. Lauren Artress, an authority on Labyrinths, points out that the seeking of answers to our questions is the act of walking a sacred path. When walking a labyrinth, we discover our sacred inner space. Walking a labyrinth is a path to our soul.

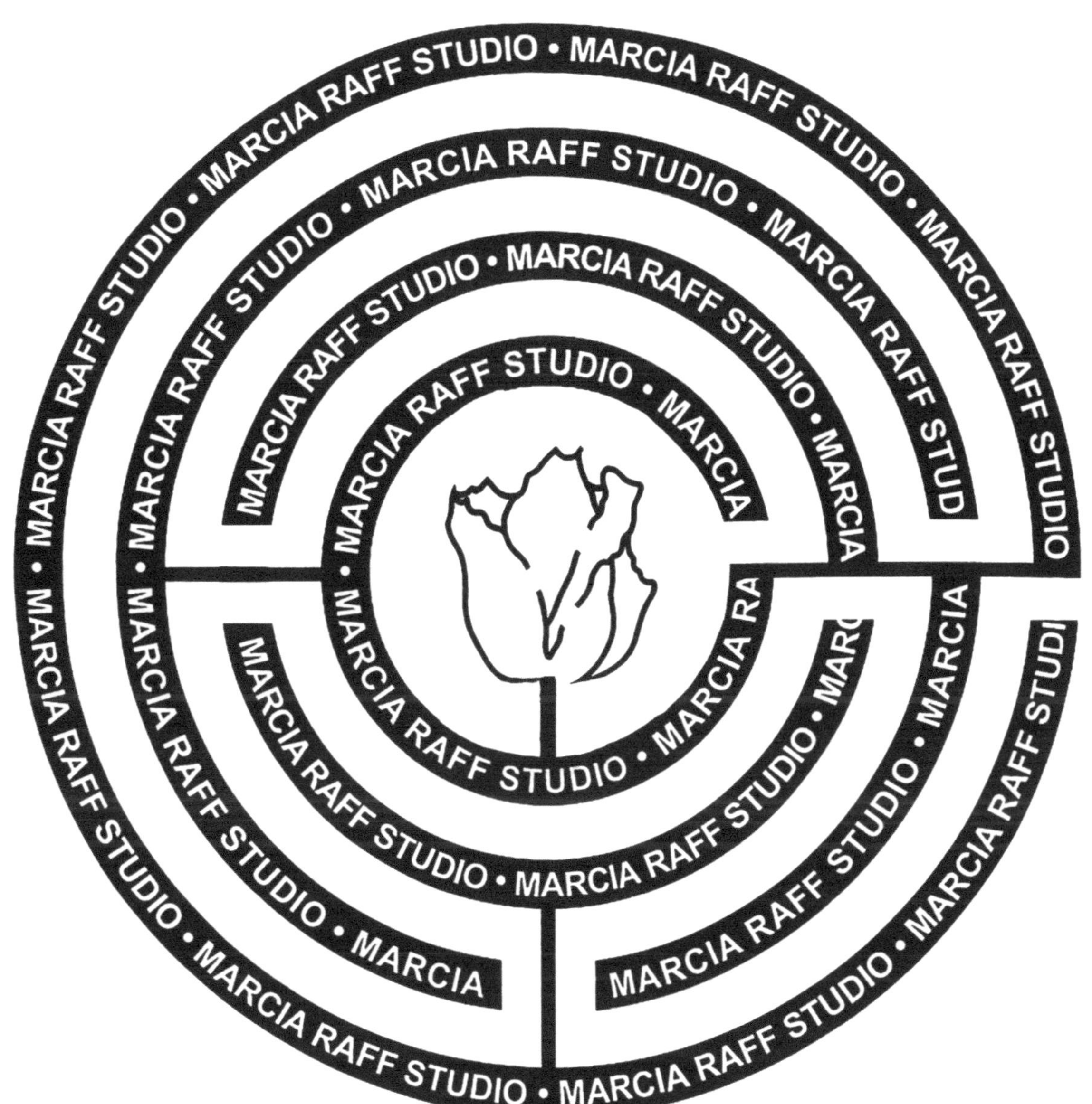

MARCIA RAFF STUDIO

I am a butterfly waiting to see,
exactly what color you will color me!

The Butterfly Labyrinth© Series 1

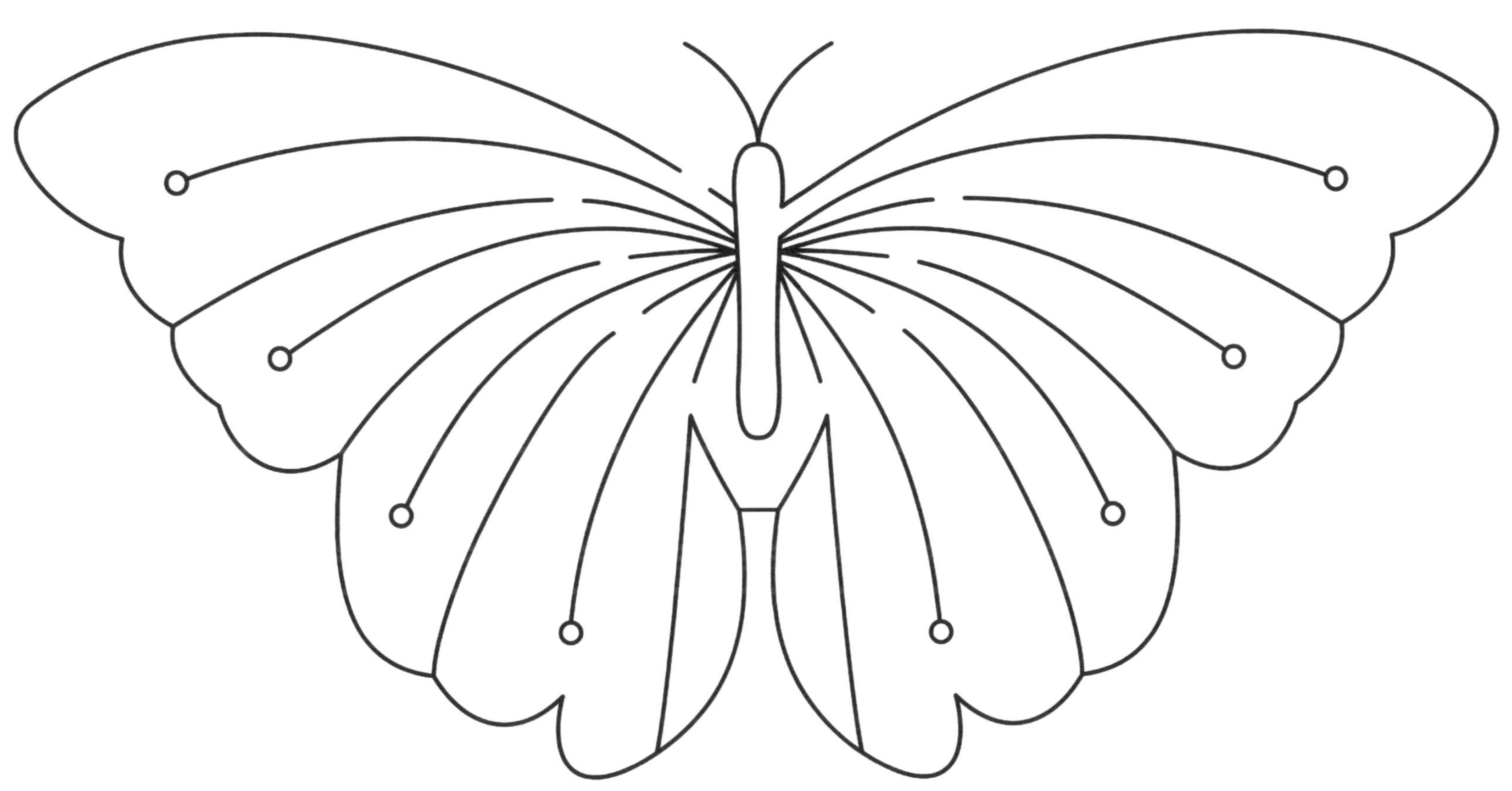

A rose is a rose that's plain to see.
I wonder what color you want me to be?

The Stem Rose Labyrinth©

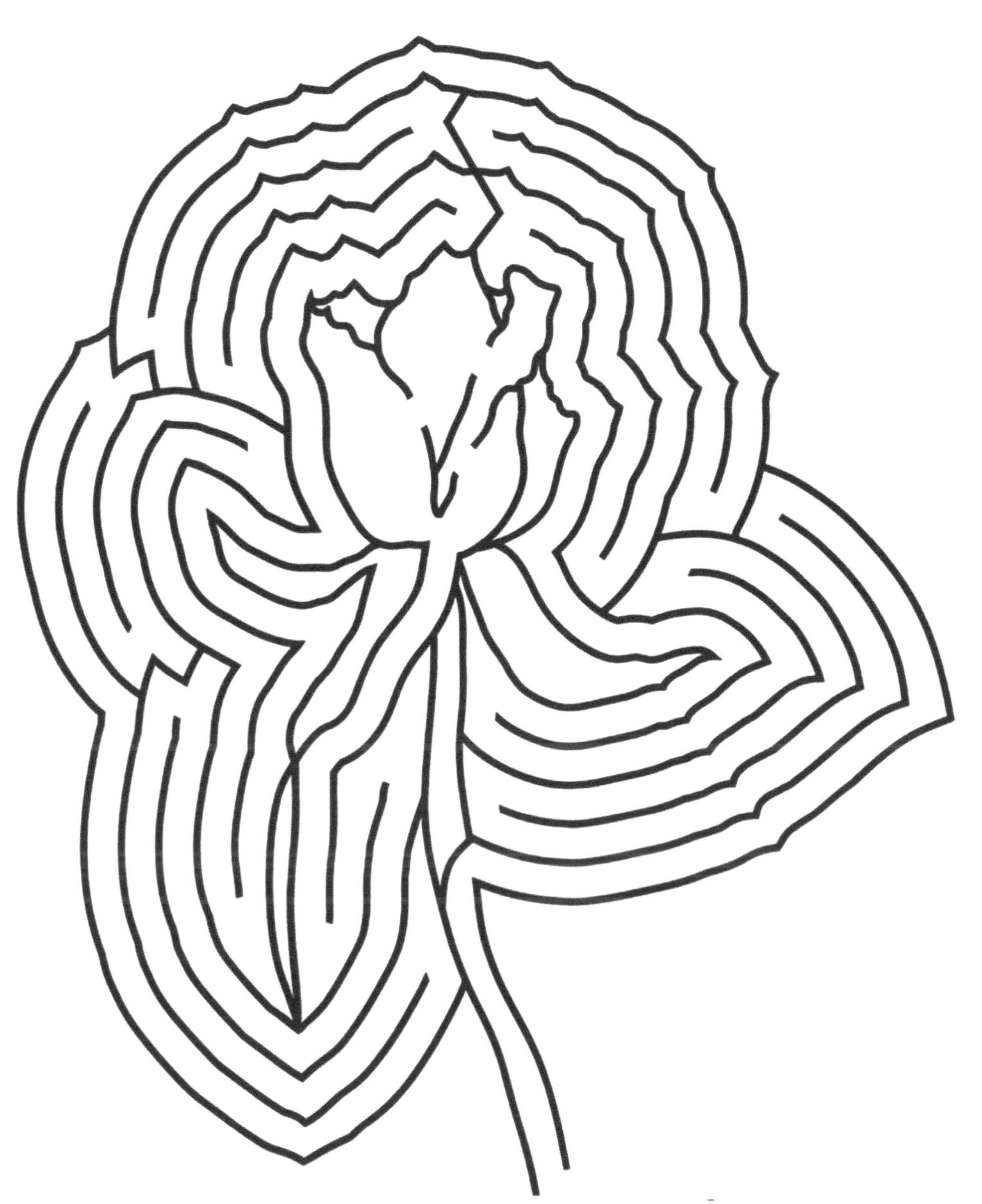

I am a Bosc pear, delicious to eat.
Whatever you color me will be a treat!

The Bosc Pear Labyrinth©

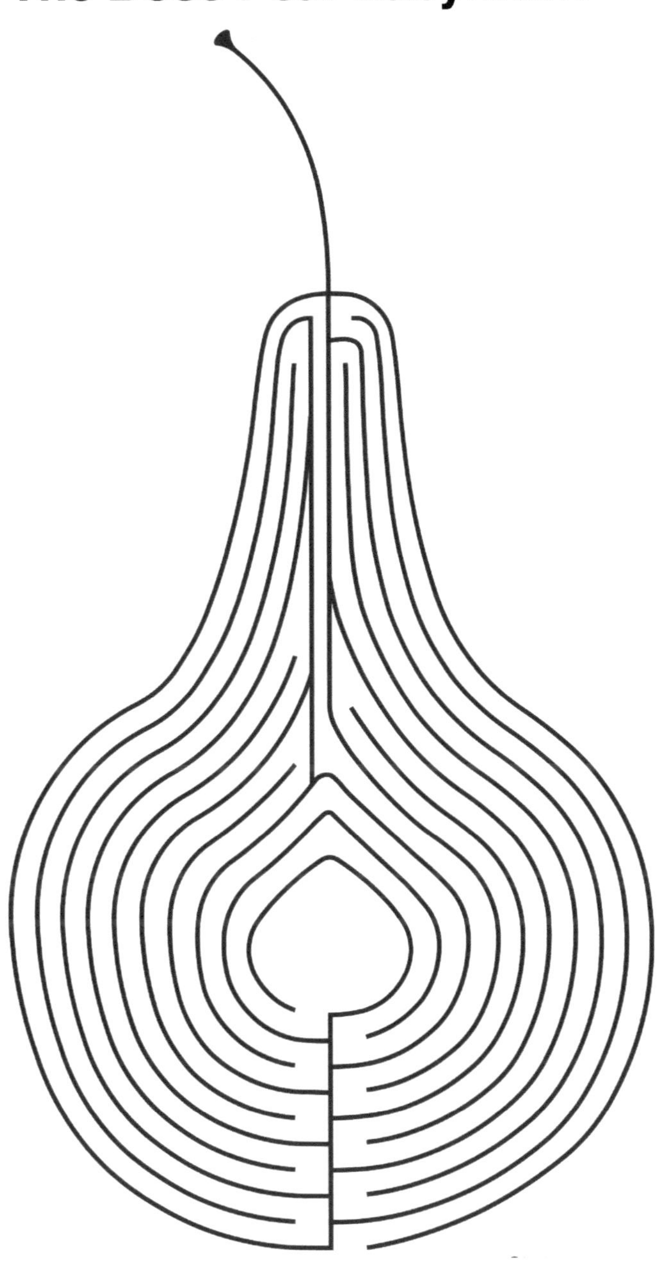

I was a beloved lion a few years ago.
Color my memorial labyrinth to make me glow!

The Mandla White Lion©

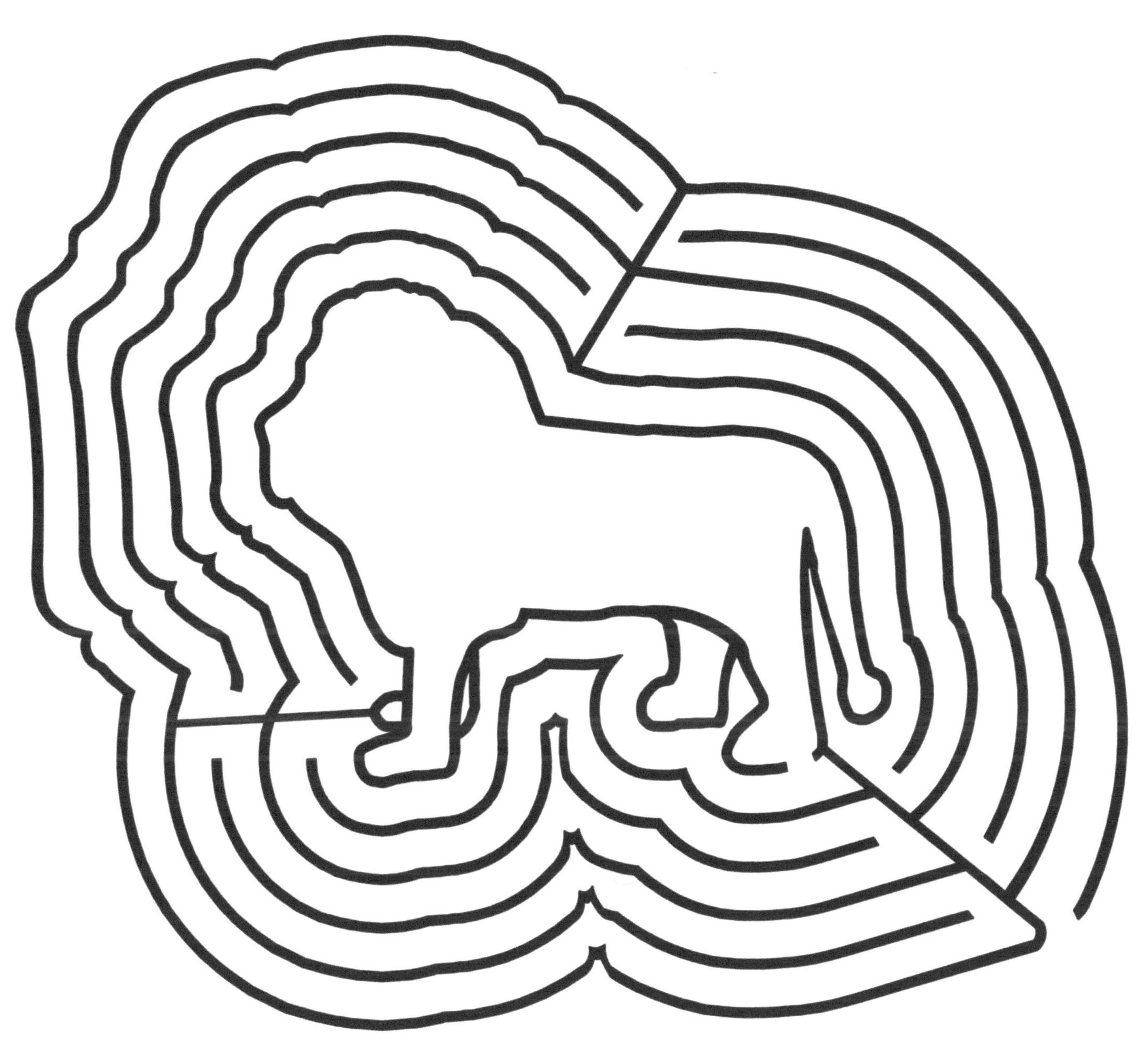

Guitars are so much fun to play!
What color will you color it today?

The Spanish Guitar©

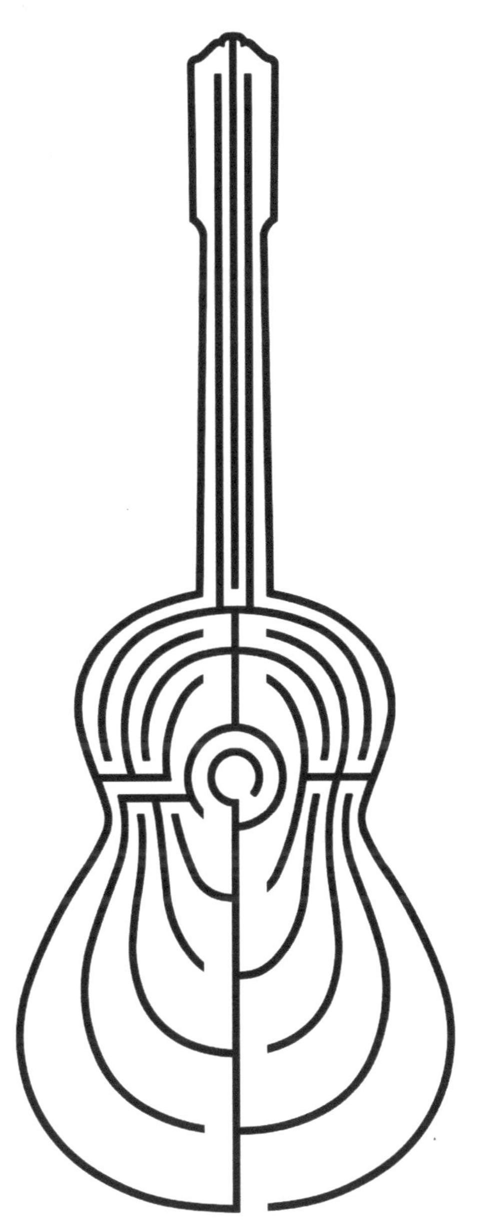

This bottle has a lovely shape, and is certainly pretty.
Not to color it would be a great pity!

The Bottle Labyrinth©

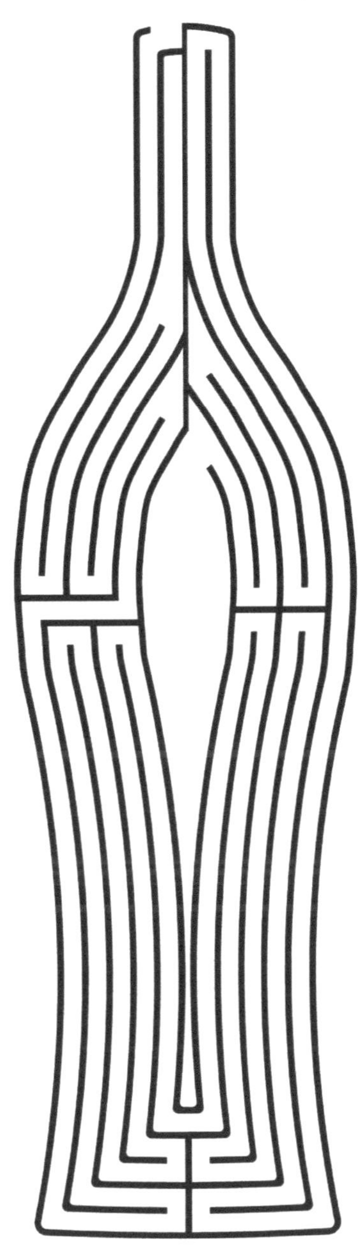

Here's a dog for you to color and name.
He's so cute and loving and very tame!

The Dog Labyrinth©

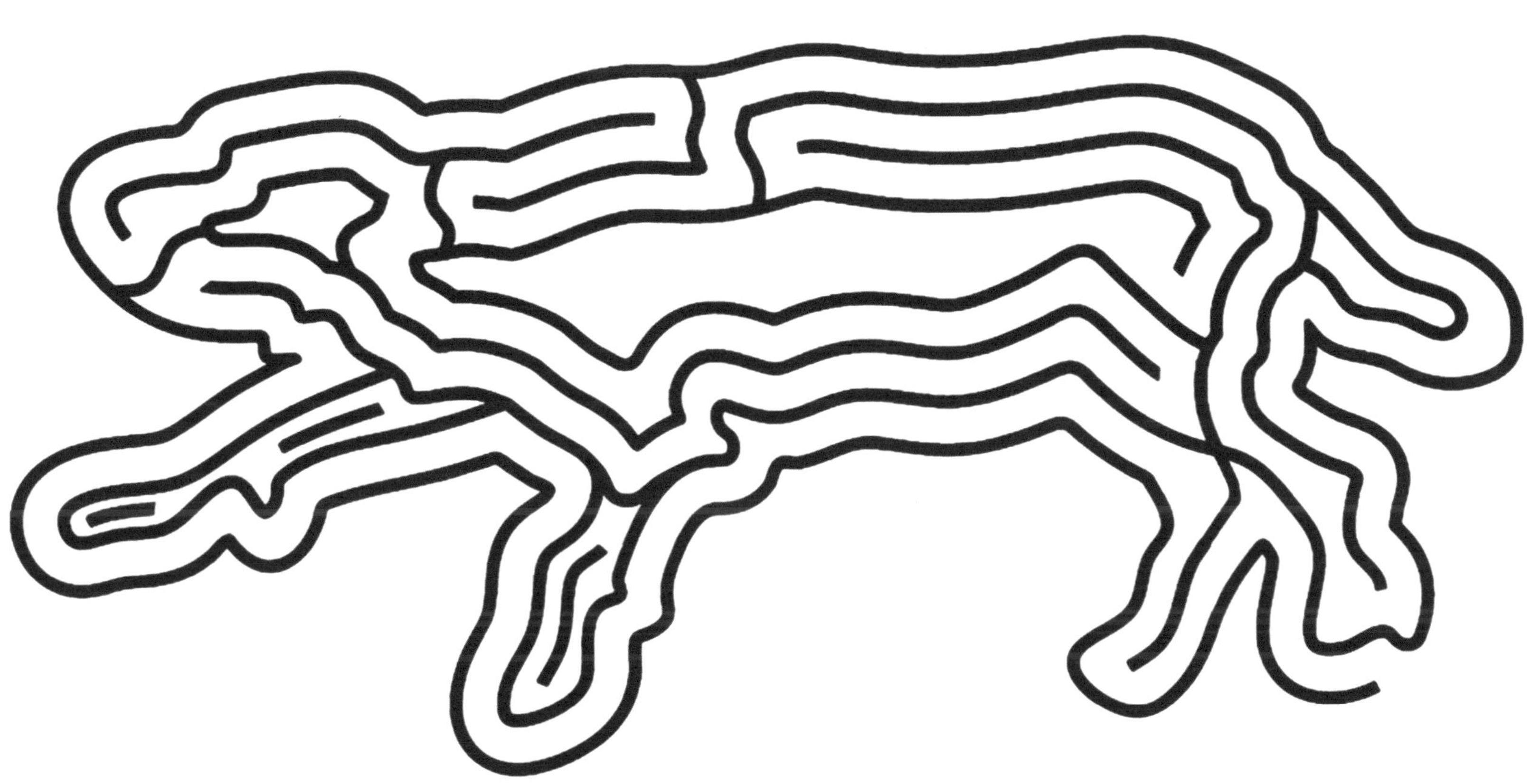

The dreidel reminds us that miracles do happen.
So put a smile on your face, and keep your fingers a-snappin!

The Dreidel Labyrinth© Series 1

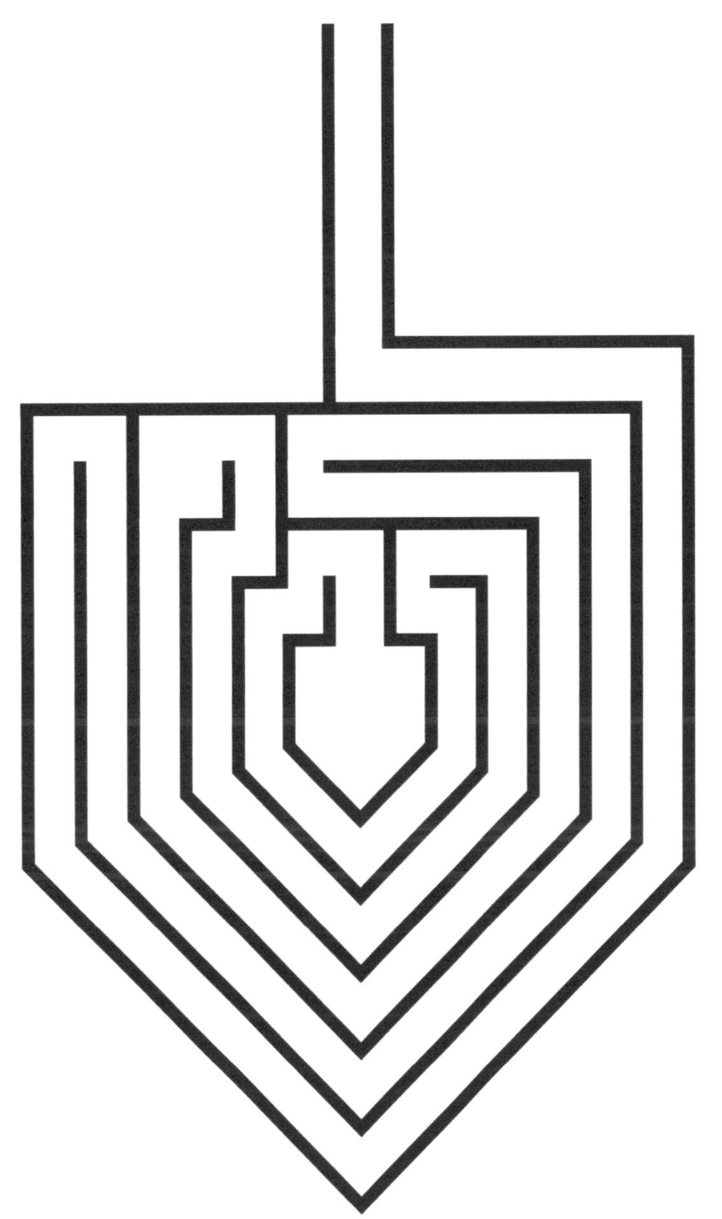

That we need love and kindness is not a myth.
Think of someone you love as you color The Peace Labyrinth©.

The Peace Labyrinth©

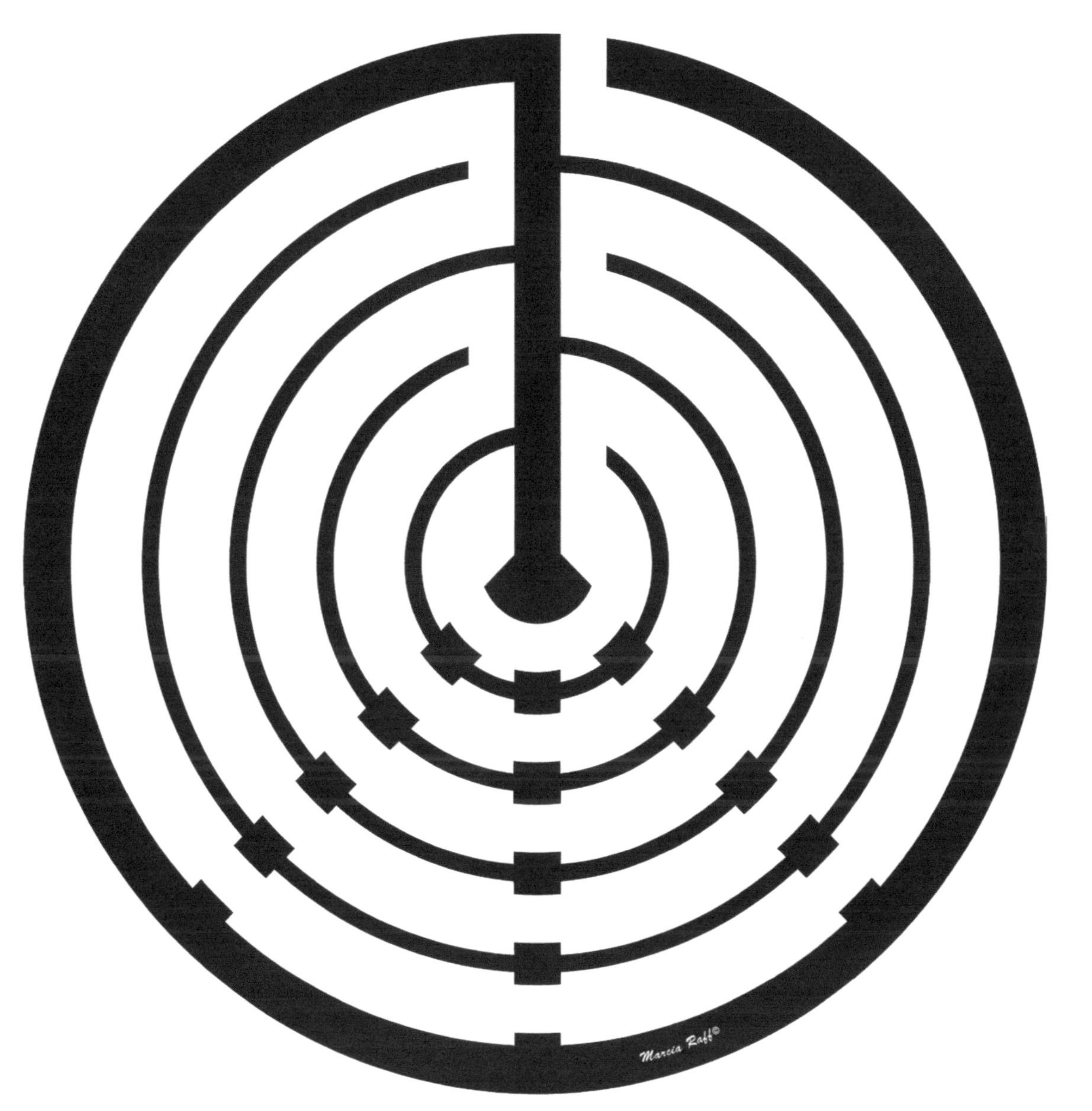

Thanks, Thanks and More Thanks!

It's been a lot of fun gathering my labyrinths so they can be walked with a finger and colored in a book. I see this book as rather simple but it took many dear friends to help me arrange it. I want to thank them for helping me from start to finish: my daughters Jill, Cathy and Amy, as well as Janice Lewis, Kay Whipple, Martha Collard, Eve Smith, Roni Lustigman, Roz Levy, Grace Lagoudakis, Shannon McArthur and Marge Weiner. I also thank my grand-daughter Shai Bar-Shany and my grandson Matthew Raff Rotchel. Everyone was kind and generous with their comments and edits. I send them all a deep bow and a bushel of gratitude. I would love to walk all of my labyrinths with them!

ISBN# 978-0-578-81724-8 Print
ISBN# 978-0-578-82221-1 Ebook

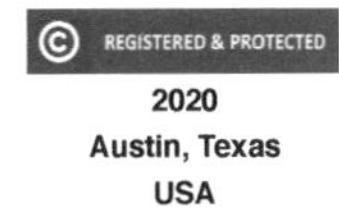